Gracious Plenty

Gracious Plenty

Michael Braswell
Foreword by Patrick O'Doherty

RESOURCE *Publications* · Eugene, Oregon

GRACIOUS PLENTY

Copyright © 2025 Michael Braswell. All rights reserved. Except for brief quotations in critical publications or reviews, no part of this book may be reproduced in any manner without prior written permission from the publisher. Write: Permissions, Wipf and Stock Publishers, 199 W. 8th Ave., Suite 3, Eugene, OR 97401.

Resource Publications
An Imprint of Wipf and Stock Publishers
199 W. 8th Ave., Suite 3
Eugene, OR 97401

www.wipfandstock.com

PAPERBACK ISBN: 979-8-3852-3684-8
HARDCOVER ISBN: 979-8-3852-3685-5
EBOOK ISBN: 979-8-3852-3686-2

VERSION NUMBER 010725

To my teachers past and present

Contents

Acknowledgments | xi
Foreword by Patrick O'Doherty | xiii
Preface | xv
Gracious Plenty | 1
What makes the world turn? | 3
Time Was | 4
Heaven's Bank | 5
Fruits of Fear | 7
Beatitudes for Divided Times | 9
Pride's Companion | 10
Darkness Hides | 12
A Reckoning | 13
False Prophets | 14
Old Men Meet in Secret | 15
Thoughts and Prayers | 16
Places In-Between | 17
Shadows and Light | 18
I Have Seen Sweet Days | 19
Morton's Treehouse | 20
Darkening Green | 21
Deception and Discernment | 22
Appearances | 25

When Will We Turn | 27
Facing Jerusalem | 28
Beginnings and Endings | 30
All Roads Lead Somewhere | 32
BAM! | 33
Speaking the Deep | 36
Plant Me Beneath the Trees | 37
Low Road of Sorrow | 38
In Times Like These | 40
Shrapnel | 41
Feeding Pigeons | 42
Sum of Hurts | 43
Father and Son | 46
The Search for Something More | 48
Questions and Answers | 49
When is enough, enough? | 52
She has dreams of her own | 53
What Lies Beyond | 54
Holy Madonna | 55
Beginner's Mind | 56
Silence | 59
Resurrection | 61
Be That | 63
The Big Change | 64
God of Thunder | 69
Forty Years or More | 71
Peacemaking Boogie | 72
Coming Home | 74
Gratitude | 76
Feeding Five Thousand | 77
M.L.'s Garden | 78

Get Ready | 81

Bibliography | 83
About the author | 84

Acknowledgments

Some of the meditations, essays and poems in this collection have been previously published in books I have authored and co-authored including *Journey Homeward, The Memory of Grace, Teaching Justice* and *Inner Corrections*.

"Peacemaking Boogie" was published in Foreshadow. "Feeding Pigeons," "Old Men Meet in Secret," and "Father and Son" was published in The Dan River Anthology."

Foreword

In the context of his latest book, it now seems fitting that my first encounter with Michael Braswell was in an airport hotel lounge from which we were departing on different journeys to different places with different agendas. "Gracious Plenty" is, in a sense, a reflection on the opportunities offered by such encounters, unanticipated moments that impact our lives and routines and the attractions of distractions. I recall being in awe of Braswell's honesty and humility at the time and that view has never changed.

This volume of poems and pearls is not, then, an "easy read" – for Braswell acknowledges throughout that life is anything but an easy journey, but rather one replete with shadows and light, sweet days and hungry, bye-roads and brambles. His reflections – on the deception of self and of others, on the fears and resentment that spawn mistrust and hate, on the refuge we seek in false pride and false prophets – are, at once, convicting and challenging. Yet his meditations and poems also show us not merely who we are but who we can be and, more than this, who God sees in us on our common journey homewards.

Braswell's poetry and meditations examine the search for meaning for which each of us may strive assiduously or even unwittingly stumble upon. For him, "the story is the thing". The byways, the interruptions, the encounters and all of "life's foxholes" are part of the gracious plenty of opportunities which life affords for choices and changes that offer the potential to bring grace and gratitude to ourself and to our fellow travelers. In recognizing that it is by embracing the Mystery of our journey, one in which we often delude ourselves that we are in control, we may yet find a "reconciling wholeness". His words are a call, not only to let go and let God, but to seize upon the plenty, where brokenness, tenderness and even despair can be epiphanies calling us to change, to action and in the end contentment.

Learning to embrace the search is at the essence of this book; acknowledging our mistakes on the way, recognizing the suffering and accepting the consequences we have brought about and seeking to walk humbly with God in loving kindness and grace to others. In searching for the answer to his question "Will the heart ever learn?" Braswell finds his consolation in finding gratitude for a life lived on such terms and the sense that "the readiness is all".

Patrick O'Doherty
Belfast, Ireland
Author of *Breadcrumbs: Hope and Other Complications*

Preface

Gracious Plenty is a collection of meditations, essays and poems that explore the challenges we face on our life's journey. How to live meaningful and purposeful lives, to *be* in the world, but not *of* it. Easier said than done. How not to be carried away by fear and sorrow or puffed up with pride and the pursuit of power over others.

Meditations and poems examine the difference between kindness and indifference, discernment and self-deception, and humility and hubris. Listening to the still, small voice and having a beginner's mind help us to remain open and transformed by what is possible as we engage changes large and small, throughout our lives. We find ourselves returning home, closing the circle, becoming more than we imagined we could be.

Michael Braswell

Gracious Plenty

Gracious plenty is worth contemplating on the long walk we call life.

From our first breath to our last, we bounce between fear and favor, desire and gratitude.

To strive to "be content in all things" is not an easy mountain to climb.

Where wealth is more important than wisdom, acquiring more important than sharing.

Where being served is more important than serving others.

Gracious plenty reveals to us that a grateful heart is a contented heart which leads to gracious actions.

Sharing what we have, no matter how meager, with others—even strangers.

Turning our offerings into unexpected abundance.

Like the boy with five small loaves and fishes whose gracious action transformed what seemed insignificant and inadequate into plenty for all.

Gracious action encourages a spirit of generosity and abundance, and a heart at peace.

A grateful heart understands the first shall be last and the last shall be first, that the order of things doesn't matter in the reconciling eye of Spirit's sight.

The way of the Spirit is not the way of the world, teaching us to be *in* the world, but not *of* it.

The way of the world invites us instead, to become *of* the world we are *in*.

Routines drive us around our lives, often providing a detour from what is possible. No need to think or imagine a different route, a different purpose.

What we become used to is in large measure what we become.

We become used to where we live, where we shop . . . and our friends. Some of us also become used to being alone and forgotten.

We can be alone, but not lonely. Our imagination can open our eyes to see the wonder that is around and within us. The conversation of trees in the park, the chorus of tree frogs at night and cherished moments of experiences long past, all reconnect us to the timeless reality we remain a part of.

What makes the world turn?

Some say love.

Others say money.

Money talks with a loud voice and makes promises it can't keep.

What do our loved ones want most, our time or our money?

We can make more money, but we withdraw our time from whatever amount has been given to us.

Our bank account may be growing, but our time is running out.

Time Was

Not too long ago
a person's word was their bond,
but it's too much trouble now,
too hard to do.
Few words are spoken—
more announcements, less conversation.
Loudspeakers tell us about the specials on aisle three
and our credit cards reply.
Time was not too long ago
people talked to each other.
Now money talks
and people listen.

Heaven's Bank

When elections roll around,
the battle cry rings out.
It's the economy and all that goes with it.
The ECONOMY, first and last, character not so much.
When elections roll around,
we want Cesar not Jesus.
We want the rich, young ruler
not the widow with her mite.
"In God we trust" is stamped on the dollar bill,
the god we trust in when elections roll around.
What profits us if we gain the whole world,
but lose our soul, our purpose for living?
That we are in the world, but not of it seems forgotten
when elections roll around, when profit and prosperity
become number one on the hit parade
and the drumbeat for justice goes silent.
In Heaven's economy things are different.
After all who needs money if streets are paved with gold?
In Heaven's bank only acts of kindness are accepted for deposit,
only cups of cool water given to those who are thirsty.
Thirsty for understanding and compassion.
Thirsty for safety and shelter, and belonging.
Thirsty for the love we can give them that was given to us.
There is no need for elections in Heaven

where the bank of grace and acceptance
is always open to all who will enter it,
including us.

Fruits of Fear

First, fear.

What follows and grows from fear's seed corn?

Fear of what others think, what others might do.

Fear of the Other—the one who doesn't look, speak, think or worship like me.

And fear that I am not respected or good enough.

If only I were richer, better looking, more talented or more successful—it must be someone's fault.

Not mine. It must be them, the ones who are different.

Fear and prejudice can ooze down the family tree from those who came before me,

inviting me to pass it on to those who come after me.

Easy enough to do. Easy enough to see it in the nervous eyes of my children.

Circumstance may play a role.

A lost job, broken relationship, or other disappointment offers me a choice.

Pick up the pieces or look for something else—someone else to blame.

Fear simmers in collective stew of grievance, glomming onto grievances of others.

My grievance becomes *our* grievance in like-minded tribe

nurtured by victimhood in spiraling conspiracy of malevolent incarnations.

Anger and protest find a voice, searching with jaundiced eye for holy cause and justification, a fire lit by hyper- nationalism, religion, race, or other extremities.

Where do I go from here?

What do I do before winding snake of grievance looks for a way to move me and the angry herd forward?

Before grievance morphs into hate and hate into acts of violence.

When I feel anger, I become anger—anger becomes me.

First feeling, then thinking, then acting.

Acting in ways I can't take back even if I wanted to.

Can I walk a different path?

To see through the eyes of the Other.

To think before I act.

Sometimes to meet in the middle.

Nuance, balance and compromise are not dirty words.

If I can never change my mind,

what else can I change?

How can I learn from mistakes,

my own and others?

The cross, gas chamber or victim hanging from a tree are rendered mute in proud passion's glittering march devoid of compassion's humility.

Can my world turn in a different way?

Where welcoming embrace of kindness and generosity of spirit allows me to become more than I imagined I could be?

Beatitudes for Divided Times

Not "Blessed are the poor in spirit, for theirs is the kingdom of heaven,"

but "Blessed are the proud, for theirs is the kingdom of themselves."

Not "Blessed are those who mourn, for they will be comforted,"

but "Blessed are the ones who do not let the suffering and grief of others get in the way

of their ambition."

Not "Blessed are the meek, for they will inherit the earth,"

but "Blessed are the bullies who take what they want for they will inherit the wind."

Not "Blessed are those who hunger and thirst for righteousness,"

but "Blessed are the self-righteous ones who persecute others who are different, always acting for their own benefit, for theirs is the kingdom of now."

Not "Blessed are the merciful, for they will receive mercy,"

but "Blessed are the ones who are judgmental and unforgiving, for they will never be at fault, always blaming others for their failures."

Not "Blessed are the pure in heart, for they will see God,"

but "Blessed are the deceivers who manipulate and take advantage of others to their own ends, for they will see gold."

Not "Blessed are the peacemakers, for they will be called children of God,"

but "Blessed are the creators of strife, the ones who sew division and anger, for they shall be called sons of chaos, retribution and destruction."

Pride's Companion

In the old days, pride was one of the seven deadly sins.

Now folks say it's a virtue.

Proud to be an American, a member of this or that race or religion or anything else we may be partial to.

There is even *criminal pride*, getting something over on someone else, getting away with dishonesty and criminal acts.

It's only wrong if you get caught.

Tee-shirts, banners and social media promote our personal brand, the high regard with which we hold ourselves and our kind.

Are we brands to be promoted or are we human beings to be experienced?

Are we more in touch with what we are grateful for or what we are proud of?

Do our children experience us placing a greater emphasis on them being kind or being popular?

False pride masquerades as pious virtue.

Excluding creates pain and grievance from those who are left out.

Including encourages understanding and respect.

Unbridled passion often renders deep wounds that compassion can heal.

Building bridges works better than burning buildings.

Hate consumes and destroys.

Love expands and makes whole.

We are all passengers in the same boat.

We are all connected, the best of us and the worst of us, in ways we cannot see or understand.

We don't control outcomes, only our intentions.

Maybe we could try harder to put our good intentions into action.

That would be a good place to start.

Darkness Hides

Darkness hides in every heart,
waiting for quickening pulse or disingenuous sigh
of a smile half given.
Reptilian tears mask the predator's gaze
with the yearning of a lover's false pride
and scent of passing lust and envy.
The moving shadow awakens,
speaking compassion and generosity
and other games of forked tongue,
offering faint praise for the damned
and the damned to come.
Will the heart ever learn
from self-righteous indignities
laid bare on altar of sweet bitterness?
Only when it breaks,
only in its brokenness
will darkness flee heart's ancient wounds.
Only in tender embrace
can hope sit lightly on a possible future,
while darkness bides its time
with patience born of inevitable return.
One way or the other,
sooner or later,
a trick of circumstance
will surprise the new day's prospects.

A Reckoning

While the world is going to hell in a handbasket
we wax eloquent about relationship angst over wine and cheese.
And clever prose describing trending themes
about "what's in", the latest cause and fashion
emblazoned on free tee-shirts if we show up on Saturday after the march.
Where are the prophetic voices with their raw, ragged prose
declaring an end to protest posturing and cocktail parties?
We should listen for desperate whispers when night falls.
Feral children riding on the edge of survival have found a way in
and rain or shine, they are coming to collect their due.

False Prophets

They come in all shapes and sizes, charisma bubbling up like fountains of malignant fantasy.

With their million dollar smiles and pearly white teeth, they offer Oscar worthy performances, affirming our complaints and assuring us that they have the answers to what's ailing us.

Our enemies are their enemies too and our heroes, theirs as well.

Only they can make things right, no one else but them.

Like pied piper of old, they make beautiful music as we follow in obedient line.

Trusting them, even blindly, to lead us out of the darkness into the light.

Only they know they way.

Trust and obey. There is no other way . . . for them to get elected to whatever they're running for or running from.

Don't worry, we are almost there. The new Eden is just around the corner.

They are like well-heeled ventriloquists who make promises without moving their lips.

Who wax eloquent to fervent followers, praying to a god they don't know.

Offering simple solutions to problems they don't understand.

There is a reason Old-Testament prophets were not part of the king's court.

They knew they could not be the conscience of the kingdom if they were in bed with the king.

Old Men Meet in Secret

Old men meet in secret

behind closed doors with shades pulled down

to plan what's best for the rest of us.

They meet in secret

to decide on war and its spoils

and make speeches and salute

the bleached skulls of the dead

as they march by in the morning sun.

Old men speak for God.

Out of both sides of their mouths they pray

and preen for a god

who wears a mask of justice and peace

that hides a thirst for blood that would make Dracula blush.

Old men weep in public

for the suffering such sacrifice requires

then meet in secret once again.

Thoughts and Prayers

Always the same
Broken bodies and broken hearts
Mass casualties lying about
Trying to escape bullets bearing their names
Or survivors Looking for small remembrance
Among debris of passing storm
Wondering if their broken pieces
Can ever be put back together again
Meanwhile back at the ranch in D.C.
Those they elected to look out for them
Are looking out for themselves
Gathering in solemn chorus on Capitol steps
To offer thoughts and prayers
Before heading to cable news
And texting urgent fundraising pleas
To stem the tide of latest fear and anger
They have conjured up
Leaving the ones left numbed with pain
With different thoughts
To wonder why they voted
For thinly disguised grifters huddled together in front of cameras
Offering prayers to make them disappear.

Places In-Between

What are we to make of the journey we find ourselves on?

It seems clear enough at first.

A baby's warmth of kin on skin, held closely like a rare jewel, each burp and giggle bringing delight to observant smiles.

Center of the universe is a nice place to be until rude awakening that others also have their turn to take.

Front of the line can quickly enough become back of the line.

Leaving the nest, rules of the road come fast. Where to stand in line, what to believe, what not to question, how to belong and not be left out.

A passion to belong, to be accepted, whatever the cost.

But maybe not.

Some choose paths less taken. Not the majority, but the curious few who take narrow foot trails into unknown lands.

Where shadows live and sometimes whispers float on evening breeze.

Where Nature reveals beauty in sunrise and sunset, and dreams spring forth in in-between places.

Like cracks in highway asphalt or deep ancient lines in the palm of a hand, each foretells what may lie ahead.

Turn right or turn left.

Stop or go.

Leave or return.

Who can know for certain?

A choice made. A roll of life's dice. An attempt to play the odds.

Unintended consequences lie waiting.

Some for better, Some not.

Shadows and Light

Light reveals hidden places,
moving through crack and crevice
of every nook and corner
in search of truth's answer
to why we hide in shadows.
Shadows are light's mistress,
offering nuanced shade to heat of a thousand suns,
as we face love's verdict
for what we have done
and left undone.

I Have Seen Sweet Days

I have seen sweet days
when all faces were welcome ones
and I was part of the world around me
Nothing to gain, nothing to lose
Nothing and everything
There have also been days
when I was the hungry child
face pressed against windows
on the outside looking in
Mirror of self-reflection turned sideways
upside down, downside up
In between desire and desolation
where sweetness flavors sorrow's regret
Where memories rise
to meet day's demands
and evening's solace

Morton's Treehouse

Where two friends sit
in shadow of an evening's light
drinking coffee and talking
about shadows and light.
For more than twenty years of Tuesdays
they gathered to wonder about
what is from what was
and what is yet to come.

Darkening Green

Twilight breathes in nightfall's descent
as darkening green exhales last light
where time in-between reveals hidden places
opening portals to distant realms
where boundaries disappear
and mind's eye sees more clearly
light embracing darkness
resting together in infinite repose
until first light awakens new days dawning

Deception and Discernment

Bumper stickers and billboards proclaim clever values that hide behind altered truth reflecting tribal rituals and propaganda.

Deception leads us to believe we can buy virtue on the cheap.

Like fake watches and sunglasses, we learn soon enough all that glitters isn't gold.

Discernment, the ability to think for oneself, to carefully consider different points of view to be able to tell the difference between what is true and what is false.

The greatest challenge is the deception we find looking back at us in our bathroom mirror.

The biggest lies we tell to ourselves.

From within and without, deception begins its dance of seduction with a smidgen of truth.

A wisp of authenticity hovers about as the lie grows into envy, prejudice, greed or some other celebration of self-absorbed deception.

Children tell the truth until we teach them to hide their feelings.

Where simply being a child is no longer valued.

It does not take long for them to worry more about what others think than what they think of themselves.

Performance not play becomes the order of the day.

Natalia Ginzburg believed we should be more discerning, emphasizing a different approach with our children and ourselves, one that focuses on "little virtues."

Courage as opposed to caution.

Frankness and a love of the truth as opposed to shrewdness, cleverness and accommodation.

Loving our neighbors and denying ourselves more than being tactful.

"To be" and "to know" more than being obsessed with success.

Sacrifices made for doing good often have no external reward.

Corrupt and evil deeds may go unpunished, even resulting in fame and fortune.

Still, we must love good and resist evil.

It is not unusual to be misunderstood and even suffer injustice for trying to do good.

It only matters that we do not commit injustice ourselves.

We would agree that Natalia Ginzburg's "little virtues" are values to live by.

That is what we would say. But what do we do?

Contradictions abound: the values we cherish on Sundays and other holy days as opposed to the way we live and work the other six days of the week.

We are taught that we should share with those in need, but Monday through Friday, "God helps those who help themselves."

On Sunday we love our neighbor. On Monday, it's every man and woman for him or herself.

How do we temper our competitive spirit with a spirit of cooperation and generosity?

Competition and cooperation, individualism and community concern, self-interest and compassion for others.

Competition with myself, not with others.

When I have done my best—all I can, that is all I can do.

Seeing myself in others, seeing them in me.

Endless desire barks at our heels breeding insecurity and mindless ambition.

Self-deception rewards our critical eye with a sense of entitlement, even victimhood.

Is life more than an infomercial offering junk food for the soul and a sweet tooth for envy?

Self-discernment leans not only into our own understanding and insight, but listens for the still, small voice that leads us toward timeless truths that bring balance and contentment.

Not the illusion of perfection, but a reconciling wholeness that can be felt and experienced more than explained and understood.

Besides, imperfection embodies its own symmetry, offering the gift of uniqueness to those who have the eyes to see.

Appearances

It is said that appearances can be deceiving.
They can also be revealing,
tell you more than you ever want to know,
burn a hole in your heart
big enough to drive a truck through.
Beautiful people appear
with practiced, perfect smiles of high fashion
and the poised prance and saunter
of those who have somewhere
important to go.
The symmetry of perfection seems boring
in an imperfect world
where there are no teeth capped pearly white
or trampoline skin.
Give me that world.
The snaggle-toothed smile
of a child's mud puddle delight
or the naïve sentiment of love's first blush
and the ancient, dancing eyes
of the leather-skinned farmer's wife.
Let me see the haunted grimace of the victim
and the hungry child holding a piece of bread
like a lottery winner.
Each, a look of beginning and ending

and every belly laugh, sigh and scream in-between.
No well-groomed mannequins in the window
or compulsive, demographically correct estates.
All is revealed in the wild places
where hauntings come in dark of night
and hope in new dawn's early light.

When Will We Turn

Great sorrow is born of love's desire
to reconcile all,
every cry of pain
and whisper of discontent
from every shape and form
of every living thing.
Love's choice existed
before time was born,
before reflections of self
in infinity's mirror
became mistaken for the real thing.
Before the itch of knowledge
and sacred power
mistook electricity for light
and intellect for wisdom.
When will we turn
toward that which bore us
through the deep
into a universe beyond our imagination,
where love's enduring invitation
beckons us still
and calls us by name
to come home.

Facing Jerusalem

How will we face our Jerusalems?
Where songs of Hosanna can turn on a dime
into chants of crucify him.
Where fickle mob can offer frenzied chorus
to praise God in one breath while praising Cesar in the next.
Even adding a "Heil Hitler" to the next demagogue who waits in line
to offer a new order and a free ride for those who worship at his altar.
With clanging cymbals, we have left quiet of Gethsemane
for the cobblestone march of onward Christian soldiers.
We have ourselves become cymbals, leaving the church in the wildwood
for the stadium chant of religion as sport and half-time entertainment.
Surrounded by preservice cappuccinos and pastries,
we hear about a god who wants to serve our good fortune
while misery abides outside our padded pews
within a stone's throw of reserved parking.
The least of us is replaced by the rest of us,
the fortunate ones who only worry about taxes and the price of gas,
not the cold and hungry, the lost children
who will trade their innocence for something to eat.
Save us from our secret vanities and stubborn grievance.
Pull our proud feet out from under us.
Silence our clanging cymbals so we can hear your voice once again.

Help us. Forgive us

Create in us clean hearts and humble spirits while there is still time

to share our bread with those who hunger,

to bind up wounds with those who care.

Beginnings and Endings

First comes birth's celebrated arrival and in the end, death's final salute, the bookends of life as we know it.

Hellos and goodbyes. First love and last love. Growing up and growing old. Coming into the world and leaving it.

From beginning to end, we live our lives through stories.

From first breath to our last, we weave the part of life's tapestry that is our own. One part fact and two parts imagination, we create revelations and remembrances about who we are and who we were.

Choices made and not made provide texture and color to stories we live, moments of courage and integrity, and moments of remorse. Leading to a point of decision, do we keep quiet or speak, walk away or step up?

Sometimes we hope no one noticed.

Either way, we remember.

Small and big regrets we try to bury are resurrected in old age. They find us even when we try to hide them.

The story is the thing. Lessons are embedded in the byways and tall weeds of our life's journey more often than on the main road. And the truth of the matter often slips in through the back door, sneaking up from behind and surprising us with delight, horror or sometimes, both at once.

Do we learn our life lessons? Do we learn from suffering we have given and suffering we have received?

Stories inform us about who we are and who we may become, reminding us of what we have found . . . and what we have lost.

Embodying the best and worst of us, our fears and prejudices as well as our hopes and acts of kindness.

Stories feed our imagination, illuminating timeless truths and sometimes, timeless lies.

Like those who have come before us, we are both heroes and villains.

In our busy-bee world, we do more buzzing than pollinating.

Meaning is more about being in time than being on time.

There is transparency on the bridge of experience between what we learn and how we live out the story that is us.

We become immersed in stories we share, filling us with wonder, even with questions that can never be fully answered.

Questions like "what is life really about?", "what is my purpose?" and "what does it mean to be a decent and moral person?"

Growing older, we wrestle with what we should do with the 'least of those' who cross our paths and come into our lives.

We wrestle with where justice meets mercy.

We live our questions more than answer them.

We wait to see what tomorrow brings, what lies around the bend in the road we travel. Alone or with others, all part of creation's revelation, a story we belong to.

All Roads Lead Somewhere

All roads lead somewhere.
Even the ones we don't know we are on.
Even the paths we believe
will lead us to a promised land.
Especially the dead ends.
Back up.
Turn around.
Head in a different direction.
The broad avenue of our youth
becomes a narrow lane in old age.
Bringing us back
to the place we started from.

BAM!

Out of the corner of your eye, you sense the truck is going to run the red light. In the nano second you froze before stepping on the gas—BAM!

You thought things were getting serious . . . in a good way. Love or something like it was in the air. Time to take the next step. Time to make your move. Except. In a hidden corner of your heart, you thought you might have heard a hissing sound. Probably your imagination. Until after the last sip of the house wine you were both drinking, someone said—BAM—"I'm leaving."

You worked long and hard for the promotion, leaving no doubt you had traveled the extra mile more than once. You deserved it. Everyone said so. Until the boss flicked a sidewise glance toward Nancy before announcing his decision. It was—BAM— the flaming flick of a dream-busting arsonist who burned you to the ground.

More than once, in one way or another, the big BAM sneaks up when we're not looking and blind-sides us, leaving a broken heap of next to nothing. Where do we go then? Where do we take our Humpty- Dumpty selves to be put back together?

Strange as it may seem, sometimes we have to be broken in order to become open.

Open to something else, something different, something we didn't expect.

Our friends can comfort us. Counselors can counsel us. Our pastors can pray for us. And physicians can even medicate us.

All of these can be good and worthy things, but in the end, still not enough.

Leaving us issues to face and personal work to do.

No one else can fill the hole we or someone else dug for us.

Sometimes we have to walk the lonesome valley all by ourselves.

Our loved ones may complement the qualities that make us who we are, but they can't complete us.

Completion, not perfection. Going inside, not looking outside.

We can start by trying to be honest.

Taking off our masks one by one.

And not pretending to be someone else.

We can quit trying to hide the lies that live in our closet until they take up all the room in our lives.

In the end, nobody cares.

Why should they?

Why should we?

We can learn to let go of what we think others think about us.

We can even learn to let go of what we think about ourselves.

We can open our eyes, heart and mind, leaving the fast lane, entering the vast lane.

We can take a different fork in the road.

Even if we are afraid, we can take it anyway.

Sure thing.

No thing.

Some thing.

The thing-ness of whatever it is, passes in time.

We don't have to go along for the ride.

We can stay put.

The Universe knows more than we do.

Clouds of misperception and confusion don't have to carry us away.

The sky remains when storms pass.

We can remain with it.

And let the big Mystery live within us.

We can see and feel deeper and wider.

Holding on with a light touch and learning to let go,

We can trust something greater than ourselves.

We can breathe.

We can be.

Speaking the Deep

I see your nervous, sideways glance,
I see your trembling hand.
You're waiting for a sign from me,
you want to understand.
I know I haven't said enough,
it could be too deep to speak.
It's all been said before
in dark of night to keep.
I know your Mama's done her best
for what I've left undone.
Bright shining for the both of us
in time's eternal turn.
Don't be afraid,
don't hide from me,
you are your Daddy's voice.
I see in you the speaker of
the Deep inside of me.

Plant Me Beneath the Trees

Plant me beneath the trees deep into the soil I came from.
Plant me beneath my leaf-bound companions
who soothed me with gentle breeze
and shade in heat of summer.
Let me listen again to their rustling sounds and singing
as I rest within their storied embrace.
Where smell of green grass comes alive after spring rains
and cascading leaves of fall color
parade through an old man's young boy's imagination.
Riding crisp edge toward season to come
where hickory and oak remain transparent through winter's gaze,
offering themselves for hearth's crackling warmth.
Grown quiet in winter's sleep,
they stretch their limbs toward promise to come
when budding beckons new birth in Spring.

Low Road of Sorrow

We will all walk the low road of sorrow at some point in our lives.

No matter how quick we are on our feet, suffering and sorrow finds us and says, "Tag, you're it."

Sometimes we find ourselves on the low road because of choices we have made. Sometimes, it comes out of the blue, catching us by surprise as we try our best to climb out of one of life's ditches.

Being betrayed, betraying the trust of another, we are all of us, at one time or another, victims and criminals of the heart.

When we are the victim, we want justice. We want the offender punished. We want our pound of flesh.

When we are the offender, we want mercy, another chance at redemption and forgiveness.

Whether we know it or not, we are all doing time in this life. How we do it depends on how well we learn from what we have done to others and what others have done to us.

We all have our homework to do.

We often hide behind secret sorrows— from pain we have received and for pain we have given.

Secret sorrows can hide a heart full of regret. Secret sorrows also hide cold, broken hearts.

Either way, the secret is the lock on the door that keeps us in the prison we have built brick by emotional brick.

Our brokenness becomes the key to the secret that unlocks our solitary grief.

We cannot get to the mountaintop unless we are willing to walk through the valley.

Do we start walking or stay put?

If our hearts are open, infinite mercy will build a bridge, a bridge of compassion . . . even when we feel we can go no further.

Jesus didn't suffer to spare us from the storms of life.

He didn't rise from the dead and walk out of the tomb to offer us a high five celebrating how well our financial investments are doing.

He didn't command us to relax in front of our big screen televisions, but to go to all people, especially the ones different from us, to share the "good news."

To be the good shepherd to others that he was to us.

To help, serve and heal the broken ones who are hurting and have lost hope.

To forgive those who are as unworthy of our forgiveness as we are of His.

In helping to heal their brokenness, we are also healed and made whole.

In Times Like These

When darkness makes itself comfortable on the horizon
And hate drip-drip-drips into casual conversation
Spreading dis-ease through exiled minds
We beg for prayer's relief
To cast out doubt's demons
And taste contentment's peace

Shrapnel

Shrapnel from childhood wounds
work their way through skin of old age
made manifest in broken dreams and faceless crowds.
What is from what was through time half-forgotten
returns to center stage in search of warm embrace,
a welcome port from sorrow's storm.

Feeding Pigeons

Sitting with his briefcase on a park bench, the old man fed pigeons.

He nodded to those who passed his way,

the mothers with their strollers and whoever else caught his eye.

When he was finally alone,

he stopped his offering of bread crumbs and sat still.

Looking first to his left and then to his right,

he bowed his head and cried large tears through shut eyes.

And then there was only the silence

serenaded by a blackbird's distant lament.

Slowly, he raised his head.

He looked first to his left and then to his right.

Wiping his eyes on the sleeve of his coat,

the old man picked up his briefcase

and went on his way.

Sum of Hurts

Your mother looked for a good man
while you dreamed about your missing father
and ironed clothes
and got supper on the stove
and took care of your younger brother.
Pretty is as pretty does,
everything in its place
where it pretends to belong
hiding secrets
and unanswered questions.
A pretty face and perfect penmanship
can hide an unhappy heart
and unanswered need
for the family you imagined others had.
Where children were not care-takers,
where laughter and smiles were spoken there,
where a daughter did not have to endure the critical gaze
of her mother's silent reprimand.
She was a princess in search of a prince
where she could take her turn in palace bed
to bask in love's glow and affection,
maybe even a Queen someday,
but not a Royal Mother.
She found her Prince, but not a Castle

and competing dreams as well
about family and children
and the downside of other's expectations,
both real and imagined.
She was unprepared for the weight of children,
never having been a child herself.
One then two, then three, then four sons—
surrounded with no escape.
The castle became a prison
and the inmates ran it.
Even if they were children,
it made her want to jump
out of a moving car.
To one after another, she gave as she was given,
a script buried in shallow grave
resurrected from her mother's ghost
where scar tissue revealed fresh wounds
speaking memories that gave no quarter.
If looks could kill so could words.
Like hard rain on a tin roof—
rat-tat-tat, they beat a steady rhythm
with a slap here and a fist there.
Still, with passing of time,
she made do with what she had
and what she had was a mix of things,
memories good and bad and in-between.
Regrets came home to roost.

She wished she had been a better mother.
She said so more than once.
To herself even more than that.
And she tried to see the cup half full,
even when she didn't believe it.
More than when she was younger,
when her regrets were something different.
She offered encouragement she used to be stingy with
and smiles more than frowns,
giving less voice to what she was afraid of,
caring less for what others thought.
Wounds not forgotten can still be forgiven.
Confession turns the page to a blank space
where new things can be written,
where the possible's whole
can be greater than the sum of hurts.

Father and Son

The father stood there, his son waiting
for one last look, one last time
in remembrance:
for 52 years of nights with his wife,
the mother of his son and daughter.
It was a magic room
where they lay together,
face to face,
back to back,
in heat and cold,
facing the wave of life together–
its coming and going–
as best they could.

And now it was time to get on with the going.
To leave the sacred place
of loving and suffering,
of growing up and growing old,
of coming and going.

The son stood there, his father waiting;
flesh of his flesh, blood of his blood,
with his mother's heart, he gathered him up
and took him home
to face with him

the wave of life,

its coming and going

as best he could.

And on the night his father left

like those "birds hauling ass when they shot them guns,"

he said goodbye.

The Search for Something More

When we are at the end of our rope and realize there are some problems money can't solve, we become ripe for change.

Our suffering points us toward humility and compassion.

Our troubled minds and fractured hearts bow before the place we find ourselves in.

Maybe for the first time, we feel for others who are suffering because now, we know how it feels.

Now, we are even free to experience care and concern for the misfortune of someone we thought was our enemy.

We quit talking.

We sit and wait—and listen for the still small voice.

We have to be still in order to know.

Although our mind's gas tank is empty, our questioning heart longs for the "peace that passes understanding."

We find strength and hope in humble perseverance, an enduring response to the pull of something greater than ourselves.

Questions and Answers

What good are questions without answers?

What good are answers without questions?

Two sides of the same coin, they provide balance in our seeking. Answers, no matter how clear or compelling, still beg the questions:

What if?

What now?

Why?

And questions, no matter their breadth and depth or cosmic inspiration, yearn for at least the hint of an answer.

The *big questions*, what should I do with my life, what should my vocation be, who should I spend my life with, what's the point of it all—are questions we wonder and think about, the ones that won't leave us alone. They are part of the Mystery we are drawn to.

We find ourselves frustrated, even exasperated, as we seek answers to questions that seem to have no answer, or at least, not the answer we want.

But is that really true?

Sometimes we have to live the question, knowing the question itself is part of the answer.

Part of the process that allows us in time to understand the difference between what we want and what we need.

Embracing the Mystery in search of answers reveals while we may be along for the ride, we are not driving the bus.

We do not have to open our eyes, minds and hearts so wide to at least suspect if not believe, that there is something in the universe greater than us; greater than our capacity to understand the invisible that lives within and beyond what we can see.

Something is going on behind the curtain of our consciousness.

We can hear it in the rustle of leaves, in the hush of twilight.

Inhaling and exhaling, there are those times when we feel the eternal breath wash over us if only for a fleeting moment.

We become aware that we do not control outcomes.

Even if we do everything right, a failed relationship, the unexpected loss of a loved one or some other personal catastrophe leaves us bewildered and lost. Our careful calculations, the premium insurance policy we purchased, and even our religious beliefs and professions are often not enough when sorrow and suffering come calling.

Every day hundreds of thousands of people like us all over the world leave for work and other activities without realizing they will not be returning to the place they call home. The goodbyes they offered their spouses and children would be the last they would give voice to in this life.

There are those moments when we have run out of time.

Our backs against the wall and the last of our hope almost gone, a thread of light pierces the dark night of our soul.

What we thought was the end can sometimes turn out to be a new beginning.

In the deepest part of ourselves, we desire an ultimate connection to the hidden order of things, a sense of relationship that will allow us to feel more at home in the world we inhabit.

We keep climbing the ladders set before us, climbing up and falling down, falling down and climbing up.

No matter how many times we try or how high we ascend, we come to know that what we seek is not a high mark of achievement, but where we are returning to.

The straight line of success we thought we wanted turns instead, to be a circle that leads us back to restoration and reconciliation with where we began.

Leaving and returning are timeless themes in our living out the big questions of our lives.

We have to leave in order to return to the place a part of us never left.

We hope for a welcome mat, not a locked door.

Asking the right questions is more important than the answers we seek.

We know less than we think we do.

It's not about how long we live or how many trophies we have acquired, but instead about how deeply we have loved and generously we have given ourselves away in service to others.

When is enough, enough?

Most of us do not receive all the love, respect and recognition we desire.

The real question is, do we receive *enough*?

While the threshold for what enough love and respect is for each of us may be different, the principle of enough encourages us to understand more clearly that a meaningful, contented life is more about what we need than what we want.

No matter what the size and splendor, a house is not necessarily a home.

We find comfort in songs like "I'll Be Home for Christmas" and recall sayings like "home is where the heart is."

Home is where our wounded hearts are cared for, where we are valued and loved for who we are, warts and all.

Where there is always a place for us at the table.

When we find our home, our striving for bigger and better will cease.

We can take a deep breath.

We have arrived.

We will have more than enough.

She has dreams of her own

She has dreams of her own
No veil of cruel indifference
or lack of common grounding
Just the breeze of possibility
for other worlds felt
In infinite stream of mystery
she goes sailing

What Lies Beyond

There is a reason for the past
for what is happening even now
and for what is yet to come
Look to the night sky
and distant star
waiting to discover
what is past
that lives on in the present
toward what is yet to come
More than can be imagined
reaching farther into the dark
than ever could be dreamed of
One cell, one heart, one being
pulsating like fireflies
on a wet summer's night
after the rain
Like stolen jewels
glimmering through space and time
illuminating eternity in their wake
All that can be seen is a flicker
a hint of what lies ahead
a memory of what is left behind
a journey too quickly past
and yet to be taken again
as if for the first time

Holy Madonna

Holy Madonna
sacred one
will you be there
when dusk falls quietly
on the mountain?

Beginner's Mind

In the beginning is beginner's mind.
Open to what is seen and what is beyond seeing.
Open to the senses and wonders of life.
Before open becomes closed.
Before standing in anxious straight lines,
learning rules of the adult road.
Curbing curiosity in order to fit in.
Losing self to majority chants and opinion.
What is lost can be found.
What has been forgotten can be remembered.
We can find our way back to beginner's mind.
A beginner's mind is not a worrying mind.
Expansive and discerning, it is open to the possible.
Not bound by self-interest or the past.
Embracing eternity's presence in timeless moment.
Our connection to the Mystery may be invisible to us, but we are not invisible to it.
Beginner's mind is quiet and observant.
Our modern minds are busy and distracted.
With a beginner's mind we can be alone, but not lonely.
We can see and feel what is around us and within us, connecting us to the infinite reality we are a part of.
Beginner's mind is a seeking mind.
Joy and sorrow, mindfully embracing what life brings our way.

To enjoy the moment without pretending it is better than it is.

To grieve loss without pretending grief is all that remains.

Beginner's mind leads us to the path we were chosen to follow.

A question worth asking: Is my life worth the price I am paying for it through the choices I am making?

Beginner's mind reminds us that our expertise is little more than a drop of water in a vast sea of knowledge.

What we know pales in comparison to what we don't know.

The Mystery remains, inviting us to continue seeking, allowing us on occasion to experience what we cannot understand.

And that turns out more often than not, to be enough.

If we can keep a beginner's mind.

Where do we start?

First comes awareness, turning toward what we normally turn away from.

Turning toward what we would rather not see in others—in ourselves.

Leaving behind the behind.

Letting go of emotion's baggage.

Learning to "be still and know."

Listening with our hearts, seeing through God's eyes and doing the work that is in front of us.

Nothing more.

Nothing less.

So how do we see and hear the work we are called to do?

We find a quiet place and sit . . . and wait.

When distractions come to carry us away, we see them, but don't follow.

We return to the quiet place and listen for the call we have been waiting for.

The one that points us toward the work that will bring us deep meaning and joy, the work that our community most needs us to do.

Silence

Silent night, Holy night.

A time to speak, a time to listen.

So listen.

Listen with my heart, with all that I am.

Listen until the still, small voice comes to me

and speaks to the deepest part of myself.

We are connected to each other, connections that are embedded in our very DNA, the past we came from and the pull toward an uncertain future.

We can have faith that beyond the veil of our not knowing, revelation's promise remains.

We open ourselves to Creation's dance.

It beckons us to come closer, inviting us to become more conscious and committed to a servant's heart.

We take communion when we share a meal with those we love, when we share their pain, when we share our possessions and resources with the stranger in need.

We take communion when we drink and eat in remembrance of those who went before us and showed us the Way.

All are part of the intimate community we belong to.

Our shared relationships with each other and the Ancient One encourage us to live out what the prophet Micah says is required of us.

That we are to live lives of integrity and be advocates for justice, especially justice for those who have no voice; to love mercy and kindness; and not be puffed up with pride, but walk humbly with our God.

We open again to the present moment, to what is happening around us and through us.

We try not to become attached to outcomes since we really don't know what the outcomes ought to be.

We think we know, but what we think can be the result of fear, insecurities and the worst of our past.

Can there be joy without the possibility of sorrow, success without the possibility of failure?

Facing the challenges that lie before us, we listen with our eyes and ears and hearts and minds to the experience we are immersed in, seeing where it takes us and trying our best to understand the truth it offers.

Resurrection

What is resurrection?

A grand passion play

or ancient sacrifice of innocence betrayed,

before rising from cold, cracked stone.

A manger foretold the tomb

where swaddling clothes smelling of burial herbs

were unable to hold back bright light of shining star

that went dark on a hill of crosses,

but not dark enough

to hide the hint of what is to come.

What is to come?

A marching band of resurrection saints,

of waving flags and golden banners

and hallelujahs exploding throughout the universe?

No marching band,

but a flute in the woods

like a whisper in leaves;

no proud trumpet and thunder of drums,

but the gardener calling one's name

or breaking bread on Emmaus Road

taking form in the formless,

here then gone.

No crescendo of chorus

or stadium applause;

only the sound of light

like a drop of sweat on the tongue from Golgotha.

Be That

We are more

than we are pretending to be.

Be that.

The Big Change

Sooner or later, each of us comes to a moment in our lives when we see a crack in the door that opens to another room.

Maybe we find ourselves in one of life's foxholes—a broken relationship, an unexpected illness or a lost job.

Or maybe on a walk in the fall woods or along an early morning beach, we breathe in the transcendent panorama of everything all at once.

Either way, the door to another room is ajar. We can choose to close it and stay put or open it and walk through.

If we choose change, we choose it with an open hand.

If we respond to change with a closed fist, it will in time, come anyway.

Where change is concerned, we can run, but we can't hide.

In our modern world, it is hard to pay attention with social media, our constant companion.

It is even harder to see what is going on in the larger landscape of our lives.

Propaganda disguises itself as news in a relentless torrent of confusing emotions and seductive misdirection.

Our inner voice offering clarity, discernment and a vision of the possible, will be confronted by a chorus of prejudice, a comforting choir that validates our fears and anxieties.

We suffer from distractions in our lives with gadgets of one sort or another.

We talk on our cellphones, but not face to face.

We look, but don't see.

We are in a hurry, but don't know where we are going. Or why we are going there.

We respond to a thousand glittering messages sent to us from our latest device.

We react, but rarely think—think for ourselves.

Kindred spirits give voice to our prejudice.

Long-buried grievances are resurrected and validated. No need to think.

We find a tribe to hoist the flag that celebrates our anger. We wait for the signal.

Charge!

Our minds closed and our emotions raw, we do as we are told.

We charge into the abyss.

It doesn't have to be that way.

When we enter the Big Change, we will find that the light is on, illuminating our path forward.

In time we will find that wisdom invites imagination and humility, moving us more deeply into what it means to be human.

Wonder and curiosity rather than certainty will draw us into the marrow of Mystery, expressing itself throughout Nature, the universe and in the human heart.

There are other kindred spirits waiting to be invited into our lives, willing to share their circle of humility, hope and good humor.

While becoming good at something can be a useful thing, it can also become debilitating. Developing expertise may allow us to see ourselves as experts based upon our accomplishments.

In embracing the Big Change, we are reminded that what we know is no more than a blip on the great Mystery's endless horizon.

If we are not willing to risk accepting the invitation to change, we will lose what really matters.

Do we remain who we have been pretending to be or do we become something new?

Do we hide behind a cloak of self-righteous delusion or do we find the wings to fly in the face of the world's reason and logic, to practice mindful compassion for those in need, for those who are least like us.

Can we learn to give voice where we have remained silent when injustice has occurred?

Can we come to see that the keeper and the kept, the offender and the victim, the parent and the child, the teacher and the student, and the incarcerator and the liberator is within each of us?

Do we have the eyes to see the disenfranchised, the hopeless and homeless who cross our paths?

Can our hearts hear their cries for help even when they remain silent?

Can we find the courage and resolve to act, to do what we can to help?

Will we be able to contain the peace and joy such sacrifice brings?

We are tempted to turn away from the Big Change. As wondrous as seeing more clearly can be, it is also intimidating, even terrifying.

When we are wrong, the conviction of Truth's clarity can cut as deeply as the comfort it offers us in our times of affliction when we are on the right path.

Even more humbling is becoming aware of the terrible cost love is willing to pay in service to others—in obedience to the truth.

The world teaches us that success and happiness are to be measured in the service we receive.

The memory of grace says otherwise.

Meaning and joy instead, come from the service we freely offer others, especially to those who are too wounded and broken to give us anything in return.

Not the fine wine at the head table the sommelier offers us and the other VIPs to sample, but the cup of cool water we offer the thirsty, forlorn stranger on the side of the road even when the stranger is us.

When it comes to service, we are a hopscotch people, jumping this way, then that.

We want to serve, but on our schedule when it is convenient.

We want to go part, but not all of the way.

We want to help, but not if it costs us too much—too much of our time or money.

We are lured by applause and recognition for the service we render.

Besides, being generous can be good for business and our bottom line.

It is worth remembering that there were no banquet tables beneath the crosses on Golgotha.

The good news is that even misfits and hypocrites like us can still serve. Even if we have stopped and started a hundred times, we can begin again.

We can listen once more to the call that compels us to move outside our own self-interest.

We can allow our passion to be transformed into compassion for those who need our help.

And we can put our good intentions into action in small and big ways, in whatever way the moment requires.

Bathed in grace and the gratitude that follows, we can experience the joy found in the truth that what we receive is greater and more fulfilling than what we give.

So how do we begin to serve others in need?

For better or worse, we are the service.

The service if there is to be any, is us.

The time for us to start is now.

The place for us to serve is wherever we find ourselves.

The only requirement for us to make a difference is that we keep trying.

We can only be concerned with the trying, trying to put our good intentions into love's action.

The rest is not up to us.

What do we know for sure, anyway?

God of Thunder

We sit in our fool's paradise
surrounded by traditions
we expect to protect us.
But the God of thunder will come
when we least expect it,
tearing our imagined certainties
into a hundred broken dreams,
a thousand empty promises.
There will be no polished pew of fine wood
or ancient cathedral spire
reaching toward the heavens.
Nothing will stop the great silent hand
from reaching into the secret places
to fracture our stained-glass hearts.
The God of thunder will come,
turning virtue on its head,
calling us to account for our doctrines of exclusion,
our rules for ruin.
We will be sent straightaway
to the hell we believe to be heaven.
Still, even in the abyss hope remains,
for past the thunder a quiet voice beckons us
in our sorry state of discontent.
To all us prodigal sons and daughters

with all of our self-righteous idols,
the God of Thunder whispers,
"Come closer."

Forty Years or More

When Moses stays too long on the mountain
we dust off idols we keep hidden in our hearts.
We strike up the band and sing and dance around false gods
who offer nothing more than a golden face
and empty promises.
And we wonder why we wander in our self-made deserts
for forty years or more.

Peacemaking Boogie

Life is short
Make a difference
Perseverance more than ability is key
Keep trying
Even when you are the victim of injustice
Even when you yourself are unjust
Keep trying
Be kind to those around you
Be kind to yourself as well
And when you are not
Keep trying
And be encouraging
Especially when there is no reason to be
Seek completion not perfection
Seek truth not power
Sooner or later the truth will set you free
But not before it beats the hell out of you
Keep trying
Answers long forgotten, the question remains:
When will the peace that passes understanding come?
Not at the end of conflict but in its midst
Peace is a long-shot
Justice even more so
Sometimes long-shots come in

Believe that they will

From peace within to peace without

From being just to justice for all

Keep trying

Coming Home

We can never quite forget the smell and feel of home.

Even if we have never really felt at home, we have imagined how it would be.

Home sweet home.

Childhood memories. Sacred memories.

Memories help keep us together in the midst of life's craziness.

Sunburned and exhausted, we find that the summer vacation, like life itself, finally winds down the road to the place from whence we came.

The house from which we were so eager to escape comes instead, to be the home which we long to return to, a place we know and where we are known.

Maybe that is what our lives are really all about—our search for a home where the welcome mat at the front door has our name on it.

Not someone else's, but our own name carefully etched, a special invitation that welcomes the me into community that is us.

In one way or another, we are all trying to find where we belong.

Who knows, maybe it is all part of the plan.

The fast-track career and good deal we negotiated may both be ways, sometimes even desperate ways, we try to create hope for ourselves on our life's journey.

Maybe if the deals are good enough, we can somehow come to feel good enough about who we are not to deal at all, to begin to feel at home within ourselves.

Still, it isn't likely to work that way.

Maybe that's why it wasn't until the prodigal son ran out of money and the world's answers that he was finally able to find his way home.

Like him, we have to face the music, accepting responsibility for the choices we have made, letting the consequences humble us.

In doing that, we can become aware that the world we live in is our home, the sky and heavens are the roof that covers us.

Nature echoes season's change, the passing of time.

Our stewardship for all we are a part of will take care of us as we take care of it.

Inviting us to become more conscious and committed to our servant's heart.

The world tells us that life is about acquiring wealth, being successful, but we know better.

We are created to serve others, especially the least of us.

We have learned that the currency of life is not money, but time.

How will we spend it?

How will it spend us?

We have learned to be content with what we have and where we are, to see more clearly with our spirit sight.

Peace in dawn's first light and beauty even in midst of life's passing storms.

Whatever our circumstance, no need to be troubled or afraid.

Nothing is missing.

We are shepherds not sheep.

We are not alone.

Gratitude

Yes, Gratitude it is.

Please pass the Gratitude this way.

Let us take an extra helping.

And then some more.

Let us practice eating and embracing Gratitude,

the fuel that sustains Hope.

Even in the worst of times—Hope.

May the winds of Grace blow freely among us

as we practice the way of service to others.

And in serving them, we come to find ourselves.

We also come to find God.

What more is there?

What more could we ask for?

Feeding Five Thousand

Dinner on the grounds

Everybody Come

Casseroles are welcome

And fried chicken

Potato salad too

Sweet tea to drink

Homemade pies to eat

Come

Sit

Eat

Share

Everyone's welcome

M.L.'s Garden

He bends to the wind
and steps as quickly as he can
always in a hurry
sometimes too much so
more to do than time allows
bumping into this and that
zig-zagging through life
touching and tasting on the run
At ninety-nine, his smell and taste are mostly gone
He creaks and cracks through failing sight
toward the place he calls his garden
white, plastic chairs positioned here and there
provide an oasis for his shuffling march
toward the distant green place
where life springs from death of winter
In his garden, corn still rises
and relish bound cucumbers grow in summer rain
and scuppernong grapes destined for jelly jars
multiply like rabbits
He breathes in morning dew and warmth of sun
and remembers again his young man's spirit
bound in time's wrinkled chains
Nothing has kept him from his garden
not hip or knee replacement nor failing heart

not even the joy of his children's children
or the friends he has grown sweet like ripened figs
or the loss of his beloved Louise, twenty-four years passed
He makes room for them all in his garden

    He's not a perfect man
    no one is
    more action than conversation
    his nervous fingers speak of impatience
    still, he's better than most
    not just in a hurry, but in a hurry to help
    with a basket of pickles, relish and jelly
    and a joke or two or a fish fry next Friday
    He's breathed his blessing
    on young and old alike
    For ninety-nine years, he's ridden life's roller coaster
    and time has come to collect its due
    while pickle and relish jars sit empty on the counter-top
    there's still grace enough for the desperate moments
    and humor enough to fill what's left to him
    in the evening of his life
    and the twinkle in his eye

    He is ready to go
    with body as dented and rusted as his old El Camino
    he likes to exhale, "No one should live this long"
    and "I've had a good life" in the same breath
    and in his case, it has been a good life
    not just for him, but for those who have known him

At ninety-nine, he's looking forward to a new suit of clothes
and directions to the green garden where Louise grows

Get Ready

Pack your things.

Get ready to leave life as you know it.

There is a new room waiting for you!

Bibliography

Braswell, Michael. *Journey Homeward*. Chicago, IL. Franciscan Herald Press, 1990 (reissued by Wipf and Stock).
Braswell, Michael. *The Memory of Grace*. Madison, WI. Borderland Books, 2018.
Braswell, Michael and Whitehead, John. *Teaching Justice*. Durham, NC. Carolina Academic Press, 2020.
Ginzburg, Natalia. *The Little Virtues* (Translated by Dick Davis). Manchester, Great Britain. Carcanet, 1985.
Higgs, Robert J. and Braswell, Michael. *An Unholy Alliance: The Sacred and Modern Sports*. Macon, GA. Mercer University Press, 2004.

About the author

Michael Braswell has published books on the Spiritual journey, ethics, human relations and other justice issues as well as four short story collections and two novels.

His books include *When Jesus Came to the Cracker Barrel, The Memory of Grace, Interview with Joab, God's Scoundrels and Misfits* and *Teaching Justice*.

His website is michaelcbraswell.com

www.ingramcontent.com/pod-product-compliance
Lightning Source LLC
Chambersburg PA
CBHW060400050426
42449CB00009B/1822